BOOKS BY OGDEN NASH

HARD LINES (1931)
FREE WHEELING (1931)
HAPPY DAYS (1933)
FOUR PROMINENT SO AND SO'S (1934)
THE PRIMROSE PATH (1935)
THE BAD PARENTS' GARDEN OF VERSE (1936)
I'M A STRANGER HERE MYSELF (1938)
GOOD INTENTIONS (1942)
VERSUS (1949)

THE PRIVATE DINING ROOM (1953)
YOU CAN'T GET THERE FROM HERE (1957)
EVERYONE BUT THEE AND ME (1962)
SANTA GO HOME: A CASE HISTORY FOR PARENTS (1967)
THERE'S ALWAYS ANOTHER WINDMILL (1968)
THE OLD DOG BARKS BACKWARDS (1972)

COLLECTED AND SELECTED

THE FACE IS FAMILIAR (1940)
MANY LONG YEARS AGO (1945)
FAMILY REUNION (1950)
VERSES FROM 1929 ON (1959)
MARRIAGE LINES: NOTES OF A STUDENT HUSBAND (1964)
BED RIDDANCE: A POSY FOR THE INDISPOSED (1970)

AVE OGDEN: NASH IN LATIN (TRANSLATED BY JAMES C. GLEESON AND BRIAN N. MEYER) (1973)
I WOULDN'T HAVE MISSED IT: SELECTED POEMS OF OGDEN NASH (1975)
A PENNY SAVED IS IMPOSSIBLE (1981)

FOR CHILDREN

THE CRICKET OF CARADOR (WITH JOSEPH ALGER) (1925)
MUSICAL ZOO (WITH TUNES BY VERNON DUKE) (1947)
PARENTS KEEP OUT: ELDERLY POEMS FOR YOUNGERLY READERS (1951)
THE CHRISTMAS THAT ALMOST WASN'T (1957)
CUSTARD THE DRAGON (1959)
A BOY IS A BOY: THE FUN OF BEING A BOY (1960)
CUSTARD THE DRAGON AND THE WICKED KNIGHT (1961)

THE NEW NUTCRACKER SUITE AND OTHER INNOCENT VERSES (1962)
GIRLS ARE SILLY (1962)
A BOY AND HIS ROOM (1963)
THE ADVENTURES OF ISABEL (1963)
THE UNTOLD ADVENTURES OF SANTA CLAUS (1964)
THE ANIMAL GARDEN (1965)
THE CRUISE OF THE AARDVARK (1967)
THE MYSTERIOUS OUPHE (1967)
THE SCROOBIOUS PIP (BY EDWARD LEAR: COMPLETED BY OGDEN NASH) (1968)
CUSTARD AND COMPANY (1980)

FOR THE THEATER

ONE TOUCH OF VENUS (WITH S. J. PERELMAN) (1944)

EDITED BY OGDEN NASH

NOTHING BUT WODEHOUSE (1932)
THE MOON IS SHINING BRIGHT AS DAY: AN ANTHOLOGY OF GOOD-HUMORED VERSE (1953)

I COULDN'T HELP LAUGHING: STORIES SELECTED AND INTRODUCED (1957)
EVERYBODY OUGHT TO KNOW: VERSES SELECTED AND INTRODUCED (1961)

BED RIDDANCE

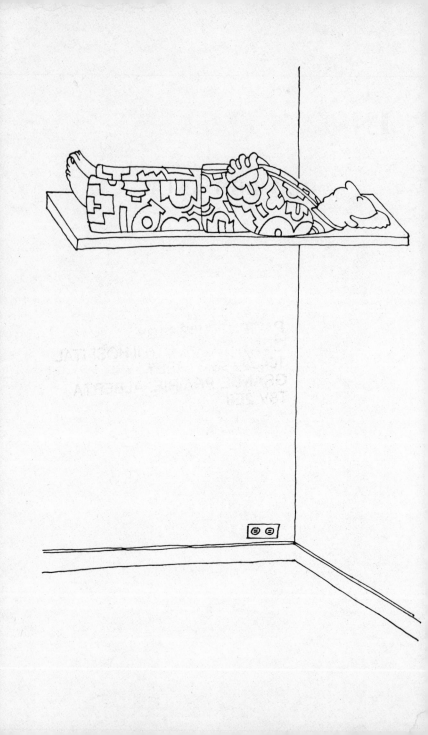

BED RIDDANCE

A Posy for the Indisposed

by

OGDEN NASH

Illustrated by

MILTON GLASER

LITTLE, BROWN AND COMPANY   ·   BOSTON   ·   TORONTO

A

Some of the poems in this collection originally appeared in
Harper's Bazaar, Ladies' Home Journal;
Look, McCall's, The New York American,
. The New Yorker and *Saturday*
Evening Post.

BP

Published simultaneously in Canada
by Little, Brown & Company (Canada) Limited
PRINTED IN THE UNITED STATES OF AMERICA

To Doctors

DOUGLAS ATWOOD

BENJAMIN M. BAKER, JR.

JOHN E. BORDLEY

WAYNE BRYER

FRANK CONSTANTINE

DANIEL S. ELLIS

GEORGE G. FINNEY

GERALD FOSTER

F. AVERY JONES

CHARLES HAHAUER

THOMAS HENDRIX

JAY I. MELTZER

LOWRY MILLER

IRVIN PAUL POLLACK

HOWARD C. SMITH

G. RIDGEWAY TRIMBLE

PHILIP WAGLEY

and the staffs of Johns Hopkins Hospital, Union Memorial Hospital, Massachusetts General Hospital and the London Clinic, without whom this book and its author could not have been put together.

CONTENTS

NOT A WINK ALL NIGHT
OR, HOW TO PASS THE TIME WHILE NOBODY ANSWERS THE BELL

WHERE DID THE POT CALL THE KETTLE BLACK? IN THE DIET KITCHEN

[ix]

A COMFORT OF COLLYWOBBLES
OR, MAYBE IT'S EVEN WORSE SOMEWHERE ELSE

VERSES FOR THOSE IN PERPETUAL
MOTION TWIXT THE KLEENEX
AND THE CALAMINE LOTION

A GAGGLE OF GRIPES
OR, I'LL BET POLLYANNA NEVER HAD A DAY'S SICKNESS IN HER LIFE

LINES TO BE REPEATED WHEN THE DIAGNOSIS BEGINS, "WE'RE NONE OF US AS YOUNG AS WE USED TO BE"
OR, MIDDLE AGE IS TOO GOOD FOR KIDS

CROSS WITH THE DOCTOR?
OR, LET'S PROVOKE A FEW ROUND HIPPOCRATIC OATHS

MUCH BETTER, THANK YOU

BED RIDDANCE

INTRODUCTION

PERHAPS you and I have more in common than you think. My doctor and even certain insensitive members of my family have often called me a hypochondriac, an accusation which I firmly if pettishly deny. My occasional moans and whimpers are forced from me not by my imagination but by the brutal fact that since my delivery date, August 19, 1902, I have been undergoing progressive obsolescence as planned by my maker, who in this respect anticipated the moguls of Detroit by several thousand millennia. We are all obsolescent; shall I be called hypochondriac simply because I am more obsolescent than most? Torpor, lassitude and procrastination have been the least of my defects. Add to these astigmatism, dyspepsia, the common cold, dreams of falling, gout masquerading as arthritis and arthritis masquerading as gout, a gnawing suspicion that the earth is slipping from under me, and an abdominal cavity that draws surgeons as the cooling spring the hart, then try to convince me that my twisted sacroiliac is psychosomatic.

When bedded by obsolescence I am subject to two emotions, boredom with my surroundings and resentment of healthy well-wishers. For some forty years I have been giving vent to these emotions in verses such as those which follow. I like to think that they are not altogether bitter, that they may even stir in you who are temporarily inactivated at home or in hospital some healing sense of the ludicrous aspect of human frailty. And I hope that you will be up and around tomorrow.

OGDEN NASH

NOT A WINK ALL NIGHT
OR, HOW TO PASS THE TIME WHILE NOBODY ANSWERS THE BELL

WHAT, NO SHEEP?

WHAT, NO SHEEP? These are a few of the 600 products sold in the "sleep shop" of a New York department store.

— *From an advertisement of the Consolidated Edison Company in the* NEW YORK TIMES

I don't need no sleepin' medicine —
I seen a ad by ole Con Edison.
Now when I lay me on my mattress
You kin hear me snore from hell to Hatteras,
With muh Sleep Record,
Muh Vaporizer,
Muh Electric Slippers,
Muh Yawn Plaque,
Muh Slumber Buzzer,
Muh miniature Electric Organ,
An' muh wonderful Electric Blanket.

My old woman couldn't eat her hominy —
Too wore out from the durned insominy.
She give insominy quite a larrupin',
Sleeps like a hibernatin' tarrapin,
With her Eye Shade,
Her Clock-Radio,
Her Sinus Mask,
Her Massagin' Pillow,
Her Snore Ball,

[7]

Her miniature Electric Organ,
An' her wonderful Electric Blanket.

Evenin's when the sunlight westers
I pity muh pioneer an-cestors.
They rode the wilderness wide and high,
But how did they ever go sleepy-bye
Without their Eye Shade,
Their Clock-Radio,
Their Sleep Record,
Their Vaporizer,
Their Sinus Mask,
Their Electric Slippers,
Their Yawn Plaque,
Their Slumber Buzzer,
Their Massagin' Pillow,
Their Snore Ball,
Their miniature Electric Organ,
An' their wonderful Electric Blanket?

I CAN HARDLY WAIT
FOR THE SANDMAN

There are several differences between me and Samuel
Taylor Coleridge, whose bust I stand admiringly beneath;

He found solace in opium, I found it in Codman's Bay-
berry Chewing Gum, at least until it started loosen-
ing my teeth.

Another difference between me and Samuel Taylor Coleridge is more massive in design:

People used to interrupt him while he was dreaming his
dreams, but they interrupt me while I am recounting
mine.

Now, if anybody buttonholes you to tell you about how
they dreamt they were falling, or flying, or just about
to die and they actually would have died if they
hadn't woken up abruptly,

Well, they deserve to be treated interruptly,

But when somebody with a really interesting dream takes
the floor,

I don't think people ought to break away and start listen-
ing to the neighborhood bore.

Therefore I feel I need offer no apology

For having gathered a few of my more representative
dreams into a modest anthology.

Once I dreamt I was in this sort of, you know, desert with
cactuses only they were more like caterpillars and
there were skulls and all the rest,

And right in the middle of this desert was a lifeboat with the name *Mary Celeste,*

And if I hadn't woken up because the heat was so blistery,

Why, I bet I would have solved this mystery of nautical history.

Another time I dreamt I was climbing this mountain although actually it was more like a beach,

And all of a sudden this sort of a merry-go-round I forgot to tell you about turned into a shack with a sign saying, LEDA'S PLACE, SWANBURGERS 10¢ EACH.

I hope you will agree that of dreams I am a connoisseur,

And next time I will tell you about either how I dreamt I went down the rabbit hole or through the looking glass, whichever you prefer.

COMPLAINT TO
FOUR ANGELS

Every night at sleepy-time
Into bed I gladly climb.
Every night anew I hope
That with the covers I can cope.

Adjust the blanket fore and aft.
Swallow next a soothing draught;
Then a page of Scott or Cooper
May induce a healthful stupor.

O the soft luxurious dark,
Where carking cares no longer cark.
Traffic dies along the street.
The light is out. So are your feet.

Adjust the blanket aft and fore,
Sigh, and settle down once more.
Behold, a breeze! The curtains puff.
One blanket isn't quite enough.

Yawn and rise and seek your slippers,
Which, by now, are cold as kippers.
Yawn, and stretch, and prod yourself,
And fetch a blanket from the shelf.

And so to bed again, again,
Cozy under blankets twain.
Welcome warmth and sweet nirvana
Till eight o'clock or so mañana.

You sleep as deep as Crater Lake,
Then you dream and toss and wake.
Where is the breeze? There isn't any.
Two blankets, boy, are one too many.

O stilly night, why are you not
Consistent in your cold and hot?
O slumber's chains, unlocked so oft
With blankets being donned or doffed!

The angels who should guard my bed
I fear are slumbering instead.
O angels, please resume your hovering;
I'll sleep, and you adjust the covering.

THE STILLY NIGHT:
A SOPORIFIC REFLECTION

He unwinds himself from the bedclothes each morn and
    piteously proclaims that he didn't sleep a wink, and
    she gives him a glance savage and murderous

And replies that it was she who didn't close an eye until
    cockcrow because of his swinish slumber as evi-
    denced by his snores continuous and stertorous,

And his indignation is unconcealed,

He says she must have dreamed that one up during her
    night-long sweet repose, which he was fully con-
    scious of because for eight solid hours he had lis-
    tened to her breathing not quite so gentle as a
    zephyr on a flowery field.

The fact is that she did awaken twice for brief intervals
    and he was indeed asleep and snoring, and he did
    awaken similarly and she was indeed unconscious
    and breathing miscellaneously,

But they were never both awake simultaneously.

Oh, sleep it is a blessed thing, but not to those wakeful
    ones who watch their mates luxuriating in it when
    they feel that their own is sorely in arrears.

I am certain that the first words of the Sleeping Beauty
    to her prince were, "You *would* have to kiss me just
    when I had dropped off after tossing and turning for
    a hundred years."

SEDATIVE REFLECTION

How doth the hippie cure insomnia?
By murmuring AMOR VINCIT OMNIA.

THE STRANGE CASE OF
MR. DONNYBROOK'S
BOREDOM

Once upon a time there was a man named Mr. Donnybrook.

∾

He was married to a woman named Mrs. Donnybrook.

∾

Mr. and Mrs. Donnybrook dearly loved to be bored.

∾

Sometimes they were bored at the ballet, other times at
the cinema.

∾

They were bored riding elephants in India and elevators
in the Empire State Building.

∾

They were bored in speakeasies during Prohibition and
in cocktail lounges after Repeal.

∾

They were bored by Grand Dukes and garbagemen,
debutantes and demimondaines, opera singers and
operations.

∾

They scoured the Five Continents and the Seven Seas in
their mad pursuit of boredom.

∾

This went on for years and years.

One day Mr. Donnybrook turned to Mrs. Donnybrook.

❧

My dear, he said, we have reached the end of our rope.

❧

We have exhausted every yawn.

❧

The world holds nothing more to jade our titillated palates.

❧

Well, said Mrs. Donnybrook, we might try insomnia.

❧

So they tried insomnia.

❧

About two o'clock the next morning Mr. Donnybrook said, My, insomnia is certainly quite boring, isn't it?

❧

Mrs. Donnybrook said it certainly was, wasn't it?

❧

Mr. Donnybrook said it certainly was.

❧

Pretty soon he began to count sheep.

❧

Mrs. Donnybrook began to count sheep, too.

❧

After awhile Mr. Donnybrook said, Hey, you're counting my sheep!

❧

Stop counting my sheep, said Mr. Donnybrook.

❧

Why, the very idea, said Mrs. Donnybrook.

I guess I know my own sheep, don't I?

∽

How? said Mr. Donnybrook.

∽

They're cattle, said Mrs. Donnybrook.

∽

They're cattle, and longhorns at that.

∽

Furthermore, said Mrs. Donnybrook, us cattle ranchers is shore tired o' you sheepmen plumb ruinin' our water.

∽

I give yuh fair warnin', said Mrs. Donnybrook, yuh better get them woolly Gila monsters o' yourn back across the Rio Grande afore mornin' or I'm a goin' to string yuh up on the nearest cottonwood.

∽

Carramba! sneered Mr. Donnybrook. Thees ees free range, no?

∽

No, said Mrs. Donnybrook, not for sheep men.

∽

She strung him up on the nearest cottonwood.

∽

Mr. Donnybrook had never been so bored in his life.

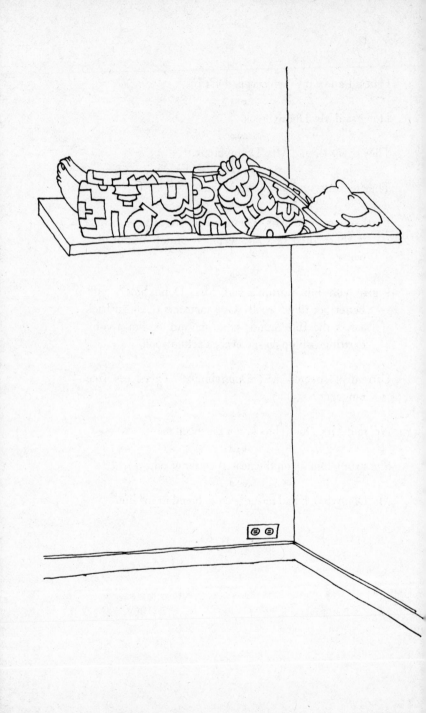

HAVE YOU TRIED STAYING AWAKE?

OR, THEY'LL FIND A WAY TO STOP THAT, TOO

Most people's downy couches have a footboard and a
    headboard,
And some people's downy couches also have a bed board.
I must tell you before I forgets
That a bed board is different from a bed *and* board, which
    is what when your wife leaves it you are no longer
    responsible for her debts,
But if you can't get to sleep because your couch is so
    downy that you are swallowed up and softly smoth-
    ered in a bottomless pit,
Why, you make it un-downy by slipping a bed board
    between the mattress and it,
Thereby earning, whether you wear pajamas or a gown,
The unusual privilege of getting to sleep by walking the
    plank lying down.
O Civilization, O Progress, O Human Ingenuity!
O Fatuity in Perpetuity!
One genius chooses downy couches to set his mind upon,
And he spends a lifetime tinkering with Angeldust and
    Fogfoam and Bubblemist until he has invented the
    downiest couch ever reclined upon,
Whereupon another genuis immediately invents a slab of
    wood that you can put under it to harden it,

[19]

And up-and-coming dealers may now feature the most irresistible of downy couches and the most immovable of bed boards simultaneously, like the poison bottle with the antidote on the label, so if I giggle in my hammock I hope you will pardon it.

WHO DID WHICH?
OR, WHO INDEED?

Oft in the stilly night,
When the mind is fumbling fuzzily,
I brood about how little I know,
And know that little so muzzily.
Ere slumber's chains have bound me,
I think it would suit me nicely,
If I knew one-tenth of the little I know,
But knew that tenth precisely.

O Delius, Sibelius,
And What's-his-name Aurelius,
O Manet, O Monet,
Mrs. Siddons and the Cid!
I know each name
Has an oriflamme of fame,
I'm sure they all did something,
But I can't think what they did.

Oft in the sleepless dawn
I feel my brain is hominy
When I try to identify famous men,
Their countries and anno Domini.
Potemkin, Pushkin, Ruskin,
Velásquez, Pulaski, Laski;
They are locked together in one gray cell,
And I seem to have lost the passkey.

O Tasso, Picasso,
O Talleyrand and Sally Rand,
Elijah, Elisha,
Eugene Aram, Eugène Sue,
Don Quixote, Donn Byrne,
Rosencrantz and Guildenstern,
Humperdinck and Rumpelstiltskin,
They taunt me, two by two.

At last, in the stilly night,
When the mind is bubbling vaguely,
I grasp my history by the horns
And face it Haig and Haigly.
O, Austerlitz fought at Metternich,
And a Mr. Nixon is Moby Dick,
Croesus was turned to gold by Minos,
And Thomas à Kempis was Thomas Aquinas.
Two Irish Saints were Patti and Micah,
The Light Brigade rode at Balalaika,
If you seek a roué to irk your aunt,
Kubla Khan but Immanuel Kant,
And no one has ever been transmogrified
Until by me he has been biogrified.

Gently my eyelids close;
I'd rather be good than clever;
And I'd rather have my facts all wrong
Than have no facts whatever.

WHERE DID THE POT CALL THE KETTLE BLACK?

IN THE DIET KITCHEN

CURL UP AND DIET

Some ladies smoke too much and some ladies drink too
    much and some ladies pray too much,
But all ladies think that they weigh too much.
They may be as slender as a sylph or a dryad,
But just let them get on the scales and they embark on a
    doleful jerremiad;
No matter how low the figure the needle happens to
    touch,
They always claim it is at least five pounds too much;
To the world she may appear slinky and feline,
But she inspects herself in the mirror and cries Oh, I
    look like a sea lion;
Yes, she tells you she is growing into the shape of a sea
    cow or manatee,
And if you say No, my dear, she says you are just lying
    to make her feel better, and if you say Yes, my dear,
    you injure her vanity.
Once upon a time there was a girl more beautiful and
    witty and charming than tongue can tell,
And she is now a dangerous raving maniac in a padded
    cell,
And the first indication her friends and relatives had that
    she was mentally overwrought
Was one day when she said I weigh a hundred and
    twenty-seven, which is exactly what I ought.
Oh, often I am haunted

[25]

By the thought that somebody might some day discover
a diet that would let ladies reduce just as much as
they wanted,
Because I wonder if there is a woman in the world
strong-minded enough to shed ten pounds or twenty,
And say There now, that's plenty;
And I fear me one ten-pound loss would only arouse the
craving for another,
So it wouldn't do any good for ladies to get their ambition
and look like somebody's fourteen-year-old brother,
Because, having accomplished this with ease,
They would next want to look like somebody's fourteen-
year-old brother in the final stages of some obscure
disease,
And the more success you have the more you want to
get of it,
So then their goal would be to look like somebody's
fourteen-year-old brother's ghost, or rather not the
ghost itself, which is fairly solid, but a silhouette
of it,
So I think it is very nice for ladies to be lithe and lissome,
But not so much so that you cut yourself if you happen
to embrace or kissome.

GO AHEAD, IT WILL DO YOU GOOD
OR, HER EYES ARE BIGGER THAN HIS STOMACH

Most of the literature of insurance to me is cryptic and
    mystic,
But when I read it I am given pause by a certain actuarial
    statistic.
Yes, just as some people are fascinated by fisticuffs,
I am fascinated by one group of actuarial statisticuffs,
Which proves that although husbands have the temporary
    satisfaction of being stronger,
Their wives live an average of four years longer.
I haven't read any reports from Oslo or the Skagerrak or
    the Kattegat,
But those are the figures from Hartford, Connecticut.
It was not always thus,
As anyone knows who has made a tour of Colonial grave-
    yards on foot or by bus.
There lies Ebenezer who at the age of 91 entered into
    the Kingdom of Heaven,
Preceded at decent intervals by his wife Abigail, 23, his
    wife Prudence, 26, his wife Martha, 31, and his
    wife Priscilla, an old crone of 37.
Please stand by to award me a sprig of laurel or a glowing
    calendulum;
I think I have discovered what reversed the pendulum.

Today's housewife has more horror of waste than under-
   standing of the innards of her mate,
And she insists that he eat up everything on his plate.
Be he fifty-dollar-a-week clerk or fifty-thousand-dollar-a-
   year banker,
He is cowed into cramming down that last three cents'
   worth of orts for which he does not hanker.
A victim of the thrift and culinary pride of his loving but
   misguided wife,
Although he is already full, he eats up everything off the
   plate and four years off his life.
The gist of the statistic may be found right there:
The empty plate leads to the empty chair.
Madam, I assume it is your desire to extend your hus-
   band's life, not to diminish it;
What's left on the plate, buy some swine and let them
   finish it.
Swine are happy their graves with their teeth to dig,
And anyhow what's four years to a pig?

I CAN'T HAVE A MARTINI, DEAR, BUT YOU TAKE ONE

OR, ARE YOU GOING TO SIT THERE GUZZLING ALL NIGHT?

Come, spread foam rubber on the floor,
And sawdust and excelsior;
Soundproof the ceiling and the wall,
Unwind the clock within the hall,
Muffle in cotton wool the knell
Of doorbell and of decibel.
Ye milkman and ye garbage man,
Clink not the bottle, clash not the can;
Ye census taker, pass on by,
And Fuller Brush man, draw not nigh;
Street cleaner, do not splash or sprinkle;
Good Humor man, forbear to tinkle;
Ye Communists, overt or crypto-,
Slink past this shuttered house on tiptoe,
And cat, before you seek admittance,
Put sneakers on yourself and kittens;
Let even congressmen fall quiet,
For Chloë is on her latest diet,
And when Chloë is straightening out her curves
She's a sensitive bundle of quivering nerves.
Me you will find it useless to quiz
On what her latest diet is,
So rapidly our Chloë passes

From bananas to wheat germ and molasses.
First she will eat but chops and cheese,
Next, only things that grow on trees,
Now buttermilk, now milk that's malted,
And saccharin, and salt de-salted,
Salads with mineral oil and lemon in,
Repugnant even to palates feminine,
Lean fish, and fowl as gaunt as avarice,
And haggard haggis and curds cadaverous.
Today may bring gluten bread and carrots,
Tomorrow the eggs of penguins or parrots,
Because Chloë's dietetic needs
Shift with each magazine she reads,
But whatever her diet, from whence or whither,
When Chloë's on it, there's no living with her.

QUICK, HAMMACHER,
MY STOMACHER!

Man is a glutton,
He will eat too much even though there be nothing to
    eat too much of but parsnips or mutton.
He will deprecate his paunch,
And immediately afterwards reach for another jowl or
    haunch.
People don't have to be Cassandras or Catos
To know what will happen to their paunches if they
    combine hot biscuits and strawberry shortcake and
    French fried potatoes,
Yet no sooner has a man achieved a one-pound loss
Than he gains two through the application to an old
    familiar dish or a new irresistible sauce.
Thus cooks aggravate men's gluttony
With capers and hollandaise and chutney,
They can take seaweed or pemmican
And do things to them in a ramekin,
Give them a gopher that has perished of exposure
And they will whip you up a casserole of ambrosia,
Which is why a man who digs his grave with his teeth's
    idea of life beyond the grave is definite,
There's a divine chef in it.
Men are gluttons,
And everybody knows it except tailors, who don't leave
    room enough at the edge to move over the buttons.

THE PIZZA

Look at itsy-bitsy Mitzi!
See her figure slim and ritzy!
She eatsa pizza!
Greedy Mitzi!
She no longer itsy-bitsy!

SONG FOR DITHERERS

I journey not whence nor whither,
I languish alone in a dither;
I journey not to nor fro,
And my dither to me I owe.
I could find a pleasanter name for it
Had I somebody else to blame for it,
But alas that beneath the sun
Dithers are built for one.
This is the song of the dither,
For viol, bassoon or zither,
Till the greenest simpletons wither
This is the song of the dither;
When regular troubles are wrong with you,
Others are guilty along with you;
Dithers are private trouble
Where you privately stew and bubble.
Come hither, somebody, come hither,
Would you care for a share of my dither?
I want somebody else to be mad at;
"Have at you!" to cry, and be had at.
I am tired of being angry at me,
There is room in my dither for three,
There is room in my dither for two;
We could butt at each other and moo;

We could hiss like the serpent, and slither
Through the tropical depths of my dither;
Like bees we could fight along beelines,
Or spit at each other like felines;
I care not who gaineth the laurel,
All I want is a foe and a quarrel.
Alone in my dither I pine.
For the sake of the days of lang syne,
For your white-haired old feyther and mither,
Come along, come along to my dither.
With no foe in my dither but me,
I swoon, I lay doon, and I dee.

A COMFORT OF COLLYWOBBLES

OR, MAYBE IT'S EVEN WORSE SOMEWHERE ELSE

THOUGHTS THOUGHT WHILE WAITING FOR A PRONOUNCEMENT FROM A DOCTOR, AN EDITOR, A BIG EXECUTIVE, THE DEPARTMENT OF INTERNAL REVENUE OR ANY OTHER MOMENTOUS PRONOUNCER

Is Time on my hands? Yes it is, it is on my hands and my
    face and my torso and my tendons of Achilles,
And frankly, it gives me the willies.
The quarter hour grows to the half hour as chime clings to
    the tail of preceding chime,
And I am tarred and feathered with Time.
No matter how frantically I shake my hands the hours
    will not drop off or evaporate,
Nor will even the once insignificant minutes cooperate.
The clock has stopped at Now, there is no Past, no
    Future, and oddly enough also no Now,
Only the hot, moist, beaded seconds on the brow,
Only the days and nights in a gluey lump,
And the smothering weeks that stick like a swarm of bees
    to a stump.
Time stands still, or it moves forward or backward, or at
    least it exists, for Harold Stassen, for Doctor Spock,
    for Simon and Schuster, yes, and for Schiaparelli,

But for me it is limbo akimbo, an inverted void, a mouse
with its tail pulled out of its mouth through its belly.

O, the world's most honored watch, I haven't been there,
I've been here,

For how long, for one small seventeen-jeweled tick, or
have I been sitting a year?

I'm a speck in infinite space,

Entombed behind my face.

Shall I suddenly start to gyrate, to rotate, to spiral, to
expand through nebular process to a new universe
maybe, or maybe only a galaxy?

But such a Goldbergian scheme to extinguish one lonely
identity seems, well, undersimplified and, if I may
say so, smart-alexy.

Oh, I shall arise and go now, preferably in a purple-and-
gold palanquin,

Borne on the copper shoulders of a Seminole, an Apache,
a Crow and an Algonquin,

And whatever be my heart's desire, be it a new under-
standing of Time or a cup of dew gathered from the
spring's first jonquil,

Why if none of the other three will bring it to me, why
perhaps the Algonquil.

THE WENDIGO *

The Wendigo,
The Wendigo!
Its eyes are ice and indigo!
Its blood is rank and yellowish!
Its voice is hoarse and bellowish!
Its tentacles are slithery,
And scummy,
Slimy,
Leathery!
Its lips are hungry blubbery,
And smacky,
Sucky,
Rubbery!
The Wendigo,
The Wendigo!
I saw it just a friend ago!
Last night it lurked in Canada;
Tonight, on your veranada!
As you are lolling hammockwise
It contemplates you stomachwise.
You loll,
It contemplates,
It lollops.
The rest is merely gulps and gollops.

---

* WENDIGO: In the mythology of the northern Algonquians, an evil spirit; one of a fabulous tribe of cannibals.
                                        Webster's Unabridged Dictionary

FROM A MANHATTAN TOMB

I know that a little verse is a versicle but I don't know if
    a little phrase is a phrasicle
But I do know that at the moment I feel too too alas and
    alackadaisicle.
What though around me is the hustle and bustle of a
    great city at its labors?
What though I am hemmed in by the most industrious
    and ingenious kind of neighbors?
What though young people are joining forever or parting
    forever with each tick of the clock?
What though Mr. Belloc admires Mr. Chesterton or
    Mr. Chesterton admires Mr. Belloc?
What though to produce the Sunday papers thousands of
    square miles of Canada are deforested?
What though in an attempt to amuse the public thou-
    sands of writers and actors and things are utterly
    exhorested?
What though young humans are getting born and old
    humans are getting deceased and middle-aged hu-
    mans are getting used to it?
What though a Bronxville husband has discovered that
    he can put the baby to sleep by reading Proust to it?
All these things may be of great moment to those who
    are concerned with them in any way,
But how are they going to help me to get through the day?

For I have had to eat luncheon while I was still sorry
 I had eaten breakfast and I shall have to eat dinner
 while I am still sorry I ate luncheon
And my spirit has been put through the third degree and
 thrown into a very dark dank dismal dungeon.
Why do people insist on bringing me anecdotes and
 allegories and alcohol and food?
Why don't they just let me sit and brood?
Why does the population swirl around me with vivacious
 violence
When all I want to do is sit and suffer in siolence?
Everybody I see tries to cheer me up
And I wish they would stop.

NEXT!

I thought that I would like to see
The early world that used to be,
That mastodonic mausoleum,
The Natural History Museum.
On iron seat in marble bower,
I slumbered through the closing hour.
At midnight in the vasty hall
The fossils gathered for a ball.
High above notices and bulletins
Loomed up the Mesozoic skeletons.
Aroused by who knows what elixirs,
They ground along like concrete mixers.
They bowed and scraped in reptile pleasure,
And then began to tread the measure.
There were no drums or saxophones,
But just the clatter of their bones,
A rolling, rattling, carefree circus
Of mammoth polkas and mazurkas.
Pterodactyls and brontosauruses
Sang ghostly prehistoric choruses.
Amid the megalosauric wassail
I caught the eye of one small fossil.
Cheer up, old man, he said, and winked —
It's kind of fun to be extinct.

DOWN THE MOUSEHOLE, AND WHAT SCIENCE MISSED THERE

This is a baffling and forbidding world of disreputable
    international shakedowns,
And reputable scientists spending their lives trying to give
    mice nervous breakdowns.
Let us treat these scientists to a constructive suggestion on
    the house:
Have they thought to try their experiments on a married,
    or at least an engaged, mouse?
This suggestion is not frivolous or yeasty;
I want to tell them about a mouse I know, his name is
    Roger, who loses his mind at a twist of the wrist from
    his fiancée, later his wife, who first caught his eye
    because she seemed to him naught but, as he puts it,
    a wee sleekit cow'rin' tim'rous beastie.
Now, it is Roger's contention that to err is mouselike, and
    being only mouse, though indeed his paternal grand-
    mother was a mountain, he is all too often conscious
    of having erred not only as a mouse,
But as a mouse's spouse,
As a result of which when he is justly chastised,
He is, as a reasonable mouse, neither upset nor surprised.
It's a perfectly natural sequence, Roger says resignedly,
    that began with Adam and Eve in the garden:

[45]

Crime, punishment, apology, theater tickets, and eventual
    pardon.

What gets him down, he tells me, is when he has erred
    and doesn't know that he has erred,

When his conscience is clear as to thought, deed, mis-
    deed, diet and word.

It is then, says Roger, that he is ready to pay the psychia-
    trist a lengthy visit,

Because he can't apologize without knowing what to
    apologize for, whereupon the coolness which chills
    him for whatever he has done that he doesn't know
    he has done grows all the cooler for the very reason
    that he has no idea what is it.

Worst of all, he adds in despair, is that while racking his
    brains to alight on what it can be that he erred about,

Why, he often loops an extra loop about his neck by
    apologizing for an error that if he hadn't apologized
    for it she would never have heard about.

So there you are, reputable scientists, it is in trying to
    recollect and expiate sins that it never knew were
    sins,

That is why a mouse is when it spins.

GOOD RIDDANCE,
BUT NOW WHAT?

Come children, gather round my knee;
Something is about to be.

Tonight's December thirty-first,
Something is about to burst.

The clock is crouching, dark and small.
Like a time bomb in the hall.

Hark, it's midnight, children dear.
Duck! Here comes another year!

A BULLETIN HAS JUST
COME IN

The rabbit's dreamy eyes grow dreamier
As he quietly gives you tularemia.

The parrot clashes his hooked proboscis
And laughs while handing you psittacosis.

In every swamp or wooded area
Mosquito witches brew malaria.

We risk at every jolly picnic
Spotted fever from a tick nick.

People perish of bubonic;
To rats, it's better than a tonic.

The hog converted into pork
Puts trichinosis on your fork.

The dog today that guards your babies
Tomorrow turns and gives them rabies.

The baby, once all milk and spittle,
Grows to a Hitler, and boy, can he hittle!

That's our planet, and we're stuck with it.
I wish its inheritors the best of luck with it.

[49]

A MAN CAN COMPLAIN, CAN'T HE?
(A LAMENT FOR THOSE WHO THINK OLD)

Pallid and moonlike in the smog,
Now feeble Phoebus 'gins arise;
The upper floors of Empire State
Have vanished into sooty skies.
Half missing, like the shrouded tower,
Lackluster, like the paten solar,
I draw reluctant waking breath;
Another day, another dolor.

That breath I draw was first exhaled
By diesel and incinerator;
I should have wakened not at all,
Or, were it feasible, even later.
Walls of the world close in on me,
Threats equatorial and polar;
Twixt pit and pendulum I lie;
Another day, another dolor.

Here's news about the current strike,
The latest, greatest test of fission,
A fatal mugging in the park,
An obit of the Geneva mission.
One envelope yields a baffling form

Submitted by the tax comptroller;
A jury summons completes my mail;
Another day, another dolor.

Once eager for, I've come to dread,
The nimble fingers of my barber;
He's training strands across my scalp
Like skimpy vines across an arbor.
The conversation at the club
Is all intestinal or molar;
What dogs the Class of '24?
Another day, another dolor.

Between the dotard and the brat
My disaffection veers and varies;
Sometimes I'm sick of clamoring youth,
Sometimes of my contemporaries.
I'm old too soon, yet young too long;
Could Swift himself have planned it droller?
Timor vitae conturbat me;
Another day, another dolor.

VERSES FOR THOSE IN PERPETUAL MOTION TWIXT THE KLEENEX AND THE CALAMINE LOTION

TABOO TO BOOT

One bliss for which
There is no match
Is when you itch
To up and scratch.

Yet doctors and dowagers deprecate scratching,
Society ranks it with spitting and snatching,
And medical circles consistently hold
That scratching's as wicked as feeding a cold.
Hell's flame burns unquenched 'neath how many a
    stocking
On account of to scratch in public is shocking!

'Neath tile or thatch
That man is rich
Who has a scratch
For every itch.

Ho, squirmers and writhers, how long will ye suffer
The medical tyrant, the social rebuffer!
On the edge of the door let our shoulder blades rub,
Let the drawing room now be as free as the tub!
Avid ankles appeased by the fingernail's kiss
Will revel in ultimate intimate bliss.

I'm greatly attached
To Barbara Fritchie.
I bet she scratched
When she was itchy.

SONG FOR A TEMPERATURE
OF A HUNDRED AND ONE

Of all God's creatures give me man
For impractical uniqueness,
He's hardly tenth when it comes to strenth,
But he leads the field in weakness.
Distemper suits the ailing dog,
The chicken's content with pip,
But the human race, which sets the pace,
Takes nothing less than Grippe.

THEN, hey for the grippe, for the goodly la grippe!
In dogs it's distemper, in chickens it's pip;
But the lords of creation insist at the least
On the germ that distinguishes man from the beast.

The mule with mange is satisfied,
They tell me in the South;
And eager kine will stand in line
To get their hoof-and-mouth;
Bubonic cheers the humble rat
As he happily leaves the ship;
When the horse gets botts he thinks it's lots,
But people hold out for grippe.

THEN, hey for the grippe, for the goodly la grippe!
For the frog in the throat and the chap on the lip;
For the ice on the feet and the fire on the brow,

[55]

And the bronchial tubes that moo like a cow.
And hey for the ache in the back of the legs,
And the diet of consommé, water and eggs,
For the mustard that sits on your chest like a cactus,
For the doctor you're kindly providing with practus;
And hey for the pants of which you're so fond,
And the first happy day they're allowed to be donned;
For the first day at work, all bundled in wraps,
And last but not least, for the splendid relapse.
So let man meet his Maker, a smile on his lip,
Singing hey, double hey, for the goodly la grippe.

THE GERM

A mighty creature is the germ,
Though smaller than the pachyderm.
His customary dwelling place
Is deep within the human race.
His childish pride he often pleases
By giving people strange diseases.
Do you, dear reader, feel infirm?
You probably contain a germ.

ONE THIRD OF A CALENDAR

In January everything freezes.
We have two children. Both are she'ses.
This is our January rule:
One girl in bed, and one in school.

In February the blizzard whirls.
We own a pair of little girls.
Blessings upon of each the head —
The one in school and the one in bed.

March is the month of cringe and bluster.
Each of our children has a sister.
They cling together like Hansel and Gretel,
With their noses glued to the benzoin kettle.

April is made of impetuous waters
And doctors looking down throats of daughters.
If we had a son too, and a thoroughbred,

We'd have a horse,
And a boy,
And two girls
In bed.

THE COMMON COLD

Go hang yourself, you old M.D.!
You shall no longer sneer at me.
Pick up your hat and stethoscope,
Go wash your mouth with laundry soap;
I contemplate a joy exquisite
In never paying you for your visit.
I did not call you to be told
My malady is a common cold.

By pounding brow and swollen lip;
By fever's hot and scaly grip;
By these two red redundant eyes
That weep like woeful April skies;
By racking snuffle, snort, and sniff;
By handkerchief after handkerchief;
This cold you wave away as naught
Is the damnedest cold man ever caught.

Give ear, you scientific fossil!
Here is the genuine Cold Colossal;
The Cold of which researchers dream,
The Perfect Cold, the Cold Supreme.
This honored system humbly holds
The Supercold to end all colds;

The Cold Crusading to end Democracy;
The Führer of the Streptococcracy.

Bacilli swarm within my portals
Such as were ne'er conceived by mortals,
But bred by scientists wise and hoary
In some Olympian laboratory;
Bacteria as large as mice,
With feet of fire and heads of ice
Who never interrupt for slumber
Their stamping elephantine rumba.

A common cold, forsooth, gadzooks!
Then Venus showed promise of good looks;
Don Juan was a budding gallant,
And Shakespeare's plays show signs of talent;
The Arctic winter is rather coolish,
And your diagnosis is fairly foolish.
Oh what derision history holds
For the man who belittled the Cold of Colds!

MAN BITES DOG-DAYS

In this fairly temperate clime
Summertime is itchy time.
O'er rocks and stumps and ruined walls
Shiny poison ivy crawls.
Every walk in woods and fields
Its aftermath of itching yields.
Hand me down my rusty hatchet;
Someone murmured, Do not scratch it.

Reason permeates my rhyme:
Summertime is itchy time.
Beneath the orange August moon
Overfed mosquitoes croon.
After sunup, flies and midges
Raise on people bumps and ridges.
Hand me down my rusty hatchet;
Someone murmured, Do not scratch it.

Lo, the year is in its prime;
Summertime is itchy time.
People loll upon the beaches
Ripening like gaudy peaches.
Friends, the beach is not the orchard,
Nor is the peach by sunburn tortured.
Hand me down my rusty hatchet;
Someone murmured, Do not scratch it.

Now the menu is sublime;
Summertime is itchy time.
Berries, clams, and lobsters tease
Our individual allergies.
Rash in rosy splendor thrives,
Running neck-and-neck with hives.
Hand me down my rusty hatchet;
Someone murmured, Do not scratch it.

The bluebells and the cowbells chime;
Summertime is itchy time.
Despite cold soup, and ice, and thermoses
Garments cling to epidermises.
That fiery-footed centipede,
Prickly heat prowls forth to feed.
Hand me down my rusty hatchet;
Someone murmured, Do not scratch it.

Hatchet-killings ain't a crime:
Summertime is itchy time.

WINTER COMPLAINT

Now when *I* have a cold
I am careful with my cold,
I consult my physician
And I do as I am told.
I muffle up my torso
In woolly woolly garb,
And I quaff great flagons
Of sodium bicarb.
I munch on aspirin,
I lunch on water,
And I wouldn't dream of osculating
Anybody's daughter,
And to anybody's son
I wouldn't say howdy,
For I am a sufferer
Magna cum laude.
I don't like germs,
But I'll keep the germs I've got.
Will I take a chance of spreading them?
Definitely not.
I sneeze out the window
And I cough up the flue,
And I live like a hermit
Till the germs get through.
And because I'm considerate,
Because I'm wary,

I am treated by my friends
Like Typhoid Mary.

Now when *you* have a cold
You are careless with your cold,
You are cocky as a gangster
Who has just been paroled.
You ignore your physician,
You eat steaks and oxtails,
You stuff yourself with starches,
You drink a lot of cockstails,
And you claim that gargling
Is of time a waste,
And you won't take soda
For you don't like the taste,
And you prowl around parties
Full of selfish bliss,
And you greet your hostess
With a genial kiss.
You convert yourself
Into a deadly missile,
You exhale Hello's
Like a steamboat whistle.
You sneeze in the subway
And you cough at dances,
And let everybody else
Take their own good chances.
You're a bronchial boor,
A bacterial blighter;

And you get more invitations
Than a gossip writer.

Yes, your throat is froggy,
And your eyes are swimmy,
And your hand is clammy,
And your nose is brimmy,
But you woo my girls,
And their hearts you jimmy
While I sit here
With the cold you gimmy.

THE SNIFFLE

In spite of her sniffle,
Isabel's chiffle.
Some girls with a sniffle
Would be weepy and tiffle;
They would look awful,
Like a rained-on waffle,
But Isabel's chiffle
In spite or her sniffle.
Her nose is more red
With a cold in her head,
But then, to be sure,
Her eyes are bluer.
Some girls with a snuffle,
Their tempers are uffle,
But when Isabel's snivelly
She's snivelly civilly,
And when she is snuffly
She's perfectly luffly.

[67]

CAN I GET YOU A GLASS OF WATER?
OR, PLEASE CLOSE THE GLOTTIS AFTER YOU

One trouble with a cough,
It never quite comes off.
Just when you think you're through coughing
There's another cough in the offing.
Like the steps of a moving stair
There is always another cough there.
When you think you are through with the spasm
And will plunge into sleep like a chasm,
All of a sudden, quickly,
Your throat gets tickly.
What is this thing called a cough
That never quite comes off?
Well, the dictionary says it's an expulsion of air from the
lungs with violent effort and noise produced by
abrupt opening of the glottis,
To which I can only reply, Glottis — schmottis!
Not that I reject the glottis theory, indeed I pride myself
on the artistry
Of my glottistry,
But there is a simpler definition with which I freely
present you:
A cough is something that you yourself can't help, but
everybody else does on purpose just to torment you.

[68]

FAHRENHEIT GESUNDHEIT

Nothing is glummer
Than a cold in the summer.
A summer cold
Is to have and to hold.
A cough in the fall
Is nothing at all,
A winter snuffle
Is lost in the shuffle,
And April sneezes
Put leaves on the treeses,
But a summer cold
Is to have and to hold,
And there is no rescue
From this germ grotesque.
You can feel it coming
In your nasal plumbing,
But there is no plumber
For a cold in the summer.
Nostrilly, tonsilly,
It prowls irresponsilly;
In your personal firmament
Its abode is permament.
Oh, would it were curable
Rather than durable;
Were it Goering's or Himmler's,

Or somebody simlar's!
O Chi Minh, were it thine!
But it isn't, it's mine.
A summer cold
Is to have and to hold.

REQUIEM

There was a young belle of old Natchez
Whose garments were always in patchez.
When comment arose
On the state of her clothes,
She replied, When Ah itchez, Ah scratchez.

A GAGGLE OF GRIPES

OR, I'LL BET POLLYANNA NEVER HAD A DAY'S SICKNESS IN HER LIFE

VISITORS LAUGH AT
LOCKSMITHS

OR, HOSPITAL DOORS
HAVEN'T GOT LOCKS
ANYHOW

Something I should like to know is, which would every-
    body rather not do:
Be well and visit an unwell friend in the hospital, or be
    unwell in the hospital and have a well friend visit
    you?
Take the sight of a visitor trying to entertain a patient or
    a patient trying to entertain a visitor,
It would bring joy to the heart of the Grand Inquisitor.
The patient either is too ailing to talk or is panting to get
    back to the chapter where the elderly spinster is just
    about to reveal to the Inspector that she now thinks
    she can identify the second voice in that doom-
    drenched quarrel,
And the visitor either has never had anything to say to
    the patient anyway or is wondering how soon it
    would be all right to depart for Belmont or Santa
    Anita or Laurel,
And besides, even if both parties have ordinarily much to
    discuss and are far from conversational mediocrities,
Why, the austere hygienic surroundings and the lack of
    ashtrays would stunt a dialogue between Madame
    de Staël and Socrates,

[74]

And besides, even if anybody did get to chatting glitter-
ingly and gaudily,
They would soon be interrupted by the arrival of a nurse
or an orderly.
It is a fact that I must chronicle with distress
That the repartee reaches its climax when the visitor
finally spots the handle on the foot of the bed and
cranks the patient's knees up and down and says,
That certainly is ingenious, and the patient answers
Yes.
How many times a day do I finger my pulse and display
my tongue to the mirror while waiting for the
decision to jell:
Whether to ignore my host of disquieting symptoms and
have to spend my days visiting friends who have sur-
rendered to theirs, or to surrender to my own and
spend my days being visited by friends who are
thereby being punished for being well.

WE'RE FINE, JUST FINE
OR, YOU'LL BE ASTONISHED WHEN
I'M GONE, YOU RASCAL, YOU

Some people slowly acquire a healthy glowing complexion
by sitting for weeks on a beach surrounded by surfers
and seagulls,
And others acquire it rapidly by downing a couple of
hefty Chivas Regulls,
But whether a healthy glowing complexion is acquired
openly or by stealth,
It is not always an indication of health.
Your life expectancy may be minus,
You are a seething mass of symptoms, from astragalus to
sinus,
But if you have a healthy glowing complexion your
friends cannot hold their congratulations in abey-
ance;
They lose no opportunity to inform you that you are in
the pink, when you are as far from the pink as something summoned up at a séance.
Truly, who needs a physician
When every friend is a diagnostician?
And as for the physician himself, who tells you that you
could go ten rounds with Muhammad Ali, simply
because your cheeks are ruddy as a pippin,

Why, I'd as soon consult Dr. Pangloss or Dr. Crippen.

I share the resentment of Shakespeare, who obviously wrote Sonnet CXL after an evening devoted to sack and malmsey,

And the house physician at the Globe congratulated him on his healthy exterior glow, when his interior was insufferably queasy and qualmsy.

Avaunt, healthy exterior glow!

"Testy sick men," wrote the indignant poet, "when their deaths be near, no news but health from their physicians know."

I can guess why Mr. W. H. was honored as the Sonnets' onlie begetter;

Mr. W. H. alone of Shakespeare's companions didn't slap him on the back when he was feeling awful and tell him he had never looked better.

SO PENSEROSO

Come, megrims, mollygrubs and collywobbles!
Come, gloom that limps, and misery that hobbles!
Come also, most exquisite melancholiage,
As dank and decadent as November foliage!
I crave to shudder in your moist embrace,
To feel your oystery fingers on my face.
This is my hour of sadness and of soulfulness,
And cursed be he who dissipates my dolefulness.
I do not desire to be cheered,
I desire to retire, I am thinking of growing a beard,
A sorrowful beard, with a mournful, a dolorous hue in it,
With ashes and glue in it.
I want to be drunk with despair,
I want to caress my care,
I do not wish to be blithe,
I wish to recoil and writhe,
I will revel in cosmic woe,
And I want my woe to show.
This is the morbid moment,
This is the ebony hour.
Aroint thee, sweetness and light!
I want to be dark and sour!
Away with the bird that twitters!
All that glitters is jitters!
Roses, roses are gray,

Violets cry Boo! and frighten me.
Sugar is stimulating,
And people conspire to brighten me.
Go hence, people, go hence!
Go sit on a picket fence!
Go gargle with mineral oil,
Go out and develop a boil!
Melancholy is what I brag and boast of,
Melancholy I mean to make the most of,
You beaming optimists shall not destroy it.
But while I am it, I intend to enjoy it.
Go, people, stuff your mouths with soap,
And remember, please, that when I mope, I mope!

I'M TERRIBLY SORRY FOR YOU, BUT I CAN'T HELP LAUGHING

Everybody has a perfect right to do what they please,
But one thing that I advise everybody not to do is to contract a laughable disease.
People speak of you respectfully if you catch bubonic,
And if you get typhus they think you have done something positively mastodonic;
One touch of leprosy makes the whole world your kin,
And even a slight concussion earns you an anxious inquiry and not a leering grin.
Yes, as long as people are pretty sure you have something you are going to be removed by,
Why they are very sympathetic, and books and flowers and visits and letters are what their sympathy is proved by.
But unfortunately there are other afflictions anatomical,
And people insist on thinking that a lot of them are comical,
And if you are afflicted with this kind of affliction people are amused and disdainful,
Because they are not bright enough to realize that an affliction can be ludicrous and still be ominous and painful.
Suppose for instance you have a dreadful attack of jaundice, what do they do?

They come around and smile and say Well well, how are
you today, Dr. Fu-Manchu?
The early martyrs thought they knew what it was to be
taken over the jumps,
But no martyr really ought to get his diploma until he
has undergone his friends' witticisms during his
mumps.
When you have laryngitis they rejoice,
Because apparently the funniest thing in the world
is when you can't curse and swear at them for
laughing at your lost voice, because you have lost
your voice.
And as for boils,
Well, my pen recoils.
So I advise you, at the risk of being pedantic,
If you must be sick, by all means choose a sickness that
is preferably fatal and certainly romantic,
Because it is much better to have that kind of sickness and
be sick unto death or anyway half to death,
Than to have the other kind and be laughed to death.

TELL IT TO THE ESKIMOS

Jonathan Jukes is full of health,
And he doesn't care who knows it.
Others may exercise by stealth,
But he with a cry of *Prosit!*
Others put up with coated tongues,
And shoulders narrow and droopy;
Jonathan overinflates his lungs
With a thundering shout of Whoopee!
Jonathan's noise is healthy noise,
Jonathan's joys are healthy joys,
Jonathan shuns the promrose path,
And starts the day with an icy bath.

I might forgive the superphysique
Contained in the Jukes apparel;
The apple glowing in either cheek;
The chest like an oyster barrel;
The muscles that flow like a mountain stream
And the nose that needs no Kleenex,
The rigorous diet, the stern régime
Of arduous calistheenex;
I can pardon most of the healthy joys,
I can pardon most of the healthy noise,
But Heaven itself no pardon hath

[83]

For the man who boasts of an icy bath.
If the Missing Links were vigorous chaps
And their manly deeds were myriad,
Must civilization then relapse
Back to the glacial period?
Humanity learns at a fearful price;
Must the lessons all be lost?
Does the locomotive feed on ice?
Is the liner propelled by frost?

One constant truth mankind has found
Through fire and flood and slaughter:
The thing that makes the wheels go round
Is plenty of good hot water.
And therefore, therefore, Jonathan Jukes,
You deserve the harshest of harsh rebukes;
You and your frigid daily bath
Are blocking civilization's path.
You think of yourself as Spartan and spunky?
So, Jonathan, is that old brass monkey.

THIS IS GOING TO HURT
JUST A LITTLE BIT

One thing I like less than most things is sitting in a den-
tist chair with my mouth wide open,
And that I will never have to do it again is a hope that
I am against hope hopen.
Because some tortures are physical and some are mental,
But the one that is both is dental.
It's hard to give your usual effect of cheery benignity
When you know your position is one of the two or three
in life most lacking in dignity.
And your mouth is like a section of road that is being
worked on,
And it is all cluttered up with stone crushers and con-
crete mixers and drills and steamrollers and there
isn't a nerve in your head that you aren't being
irked on.
Oh, some people are unfortunate enough to be strung
up by thumbs,
And others have things done to their gums,
And your teeth are supposed to be being polished,
But you have reason to believe they are being demol-
ished,
And the circumstance that adds most to your terror
Is that it's all done with a mirror,

Because what prospect could be worser, because how can you be sure when the dentist takes his crowbar in one hand and mirror in the other he won't get mixed up, the way you do when you try to tie a bow tie with the aid of a mirror, and forget that left is right and *vice versa?*

And then at last he says That will be all; but it isn't because he then coats your mouth from cellar to roof

With something that I suspect is generally used to put a shine on a horse's hoof,

And you totter to your feet and think, Well it's all over now and after all it was only this once,

And he says come back in three monce.

And this, O Fate, is I think the most vicious circle that thou ever sentest,

That Man has to go continually to the dentist to keep his teeth in good condition when the chief reason he wants his teeth in good condition is so that he won't have to go to the dentist.

A CLEAN CONSCIENCE
NEVER RELAXES

There is an emotion to which we are most of us adduced,
But it is one which I refuse to boost.
It is harrowing, browbeating, and brutal,
Besides which it is futile.
I am referring, of course,
To remorse.
Remorse is a violent dyspepsia of the mind,
But is very difficult to treat because it cannot even be
defined,
Because everything is not gold that glisters and everything
is not a tear that glistens,
And one man's remorse is another man's reminiscence,
So the truth is that as far as improving the world is con-
cerned, remose is a duffer,
Because the wrong people suffer,
Because the very fact that they suffer from remorse
proves they are innocuous,
Yes indeed, it is the man remorse passes over completely
who is the virulent streptococcuous.
Do you think that when Nero threw a martyr to the
lions remorse enveloped him like an affinity?
Why, the only remorse in the whole Colosseum was felt
by the martyr who was reproaching himself for
having dozed through the sermon on the second
Sunday after Trinity.

So I think remorse ought to stop biting the consciences
    that feed it,
And I think the Kremlin ought to work out some plan
    for taking it away from those who have it and giving
    it to those who need it.

PLATITUDINOUS REFLECTION

A good deal of superciliousness
Is based on biliousness.
People seem to be proud as peacocks
Of any infirmity, be it hives or dementia praecox.

LINES TO BE REPEATED WHEN THE DIAGNOSIS BEGINS, "WE'RE NONE OF US AS YOUNG AS WE USED TO BE"

OR, MIDDLE AGE IS TOO GOOD FOR KIDS

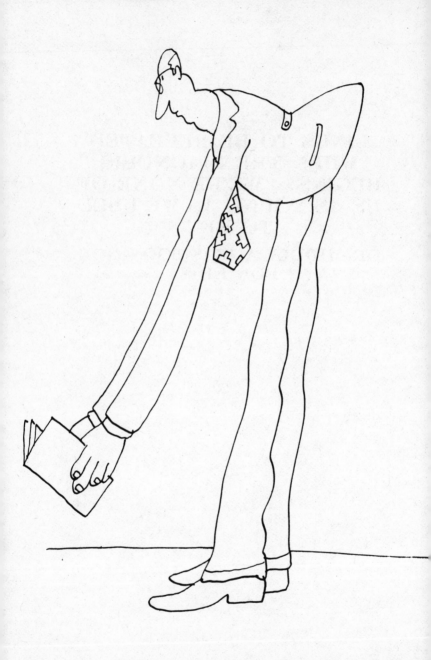

PEEKABOO, I ALMOST
SEE YOU

Middle-aged life is merry, and I love to lead it,

But there comes a day when your eyes are all right but
   your arm isn't long enough to hold the telephone
   book where you can read it,

And your friends get jocular, so you go to the oculist,

And of all your friends he is the joculist,

So over his facetiousness let us skim,

Only noting that he has been waiting for you ever since
   you said good evening to his grandfather clock
   under the impression that it was him,

And you look at his chart and it says SHRDLU
   QWERTYOP, and you say Well, why SHRD-
   NTLU QWERTYOP? and he says one set of
   glasses won't do.

You need two,

One for reading Erle Stanley Gardner's Perry Mason and
   Keats's "Endymion" with,

And the other for walking around without saying Hello to
   strange wymion with.

So you spend your time taking off your seeing glasses to
   put on your reading glasses, and then remembering
   that your reading glasses are upstairs or in the car,

And then you can't find your seeing glasses again because
without them you can't see where they are.
Enough of such mishaps, they would try the patience of
an ox,
I prefer to forget both pairs of glasses and pass my declin-
ing years saluting strange women and grandfather
clocks.

EHEU! FUGACES
OR, WHAT A DIFFERENCE A LOT OF
DAYS MAKE

When I was seventeen or so,
I scoffed at moneygrubbers.
I had a cold contempt for dough,
And I wouldn't wear my rubbers.
No aspirin I took for pains,
For pests no citronella,
And in the Aprilest of rains
I carried no umbrella.

When I was young I was Sidney Carton,
Proudly clad in a Spartan tartan.
Today I'd be, if I were able,
Just healthy, wealthy, and comfortable.

When I was young I would not yield
To comforters and bed socks,
In dreams I covered center field
For the Giants or the Red Sox.
I wished to wander hence and thence,
From diamond mine to goldfield,
Or piloting a Blitzen Benz,
Outdistance Barney Oldfield.

When I subscribed to *The Youth's Companion*
I longed to become a second D'Artagnan.
Today I desire a more modest label:
He's healthy, wealthy, and comfortable.

When I was pushing seventeen,
I hoped to bag a Saracen;
Today should one invade the scene,
I'd simply find it embaracen.

Ah, Postumus, no wild duck I,
But just a waddling puddle duck,
So here's farewell to the open sky
From a middle-aged fuddy-duddle duck.

When I was young I was Roland and Oliver,
Nathan Hale and Simón Bolívar.
Today I would rather sidestep trouble,
And be healthy, wealthy, and comfortubble.

LET'S NOT CLIMB THE WASHINGTON MONUMENT TONIGHT

Listen, children, if you'll only stop throwing peanuts and
    bananas into my cage,
I'll tell you the facts of middle age.
Middle age is when you've met so many people that every
    new person you meet reminds you of someone else,
And when golfers' stomachs escape either over or under
    their belts.
It is when you find all halfbacks anthropoidal
And all vocalists adenoidal.
It is when nobody will speak loud enough for you to hear,
And you go to the ball game and notice that even the
    umpires are getting younger every year.
It's when you gulp oysters without bothering to look for
    pearls,
And your offspring cannot but snicker when you refer to
    your classmates as boys and your bridge partners as
    girls.
It is when you wouldn't visit Gina Lollobrigida or the
    Aga Khan if it meant sleeping on a sofa or a cot,
And your most exciting moment is when your shoelace
    gets tangled and you wonder whether if you yank it,
    it will come clean or harden into a concrete knot.
Also, it seems simpler just to go to bed than to replace a
    fuse,

Because actually you'd rather wait for the morning paper
    than listen to the eleven o'clock news,
And Al Capone and Babe Ruth and Scott Fitzgerald are
    as remote as the Roman emperors,
And you spend your Saturday afternoons buying wedding
    presents for the daughters of your contemporers.
Well, who wants to be young anyhow, any idiot born in
    the last forty years can be young, and besides forty-
    five isn't really old, it's right on the border;
At least, unless the elevator's out of order.

UP FROM THE EGG:
THE CONFESSIONS OF A
NUTHATCH AVOIDER

Bird watchers top my honors list.
I aimed to be one, but I missed.
Since I'm both myopic and astigmatic,
My aim turned out to be erratic,
And I, bespectacled and binocular,
Exposed myself to comment jocular.
We don't need too much birdlore, do we,
To tell a flamingo from a towhee;
Yet I cannot, and never will,
Unless the silly birds stand still.
And there's no enlightenment so obscure
As ornithological literature.
Is yon strange creature a common chickadee,
Or a migrant *alouette* from Picardy?
You rush to consult your Nature guide
And inspect the gallery inside,
But a bird in the open never looks
Like its picture in the birdie books —
Or if it once did, it has changed its plumage,
And plunges you back into ignorant gloomage.
That is why I sit here growing old by inches,
Watching the clock instead of finches,
But I sometimes visualize in my gin
The Audubon that I audubin.

[99]

BIRTHDAY ON THE BEACH

At another year
I would not boggle,
Except that when I jog
I joggle.

AND HOW KEEN WAS THE VISION OF SIR LAUNFAL?

Man's earliest pastime, I suppose,
Was to play with his fingers and his toes.
Then later, wearying of himself,
He devised the monster and the elf,
Enlivening his existence drab
With Blunderbore and Puck and Mab.
A modern man, in modern Maryland,
I boast my private gate to fairyland,
My kaleidoscope, my cornucopia,
My own philosopher's stone, myopia.
Except when rationalized by lenses,
My world is not what other men's is;
Unless I have my glasses on,
The postman is a leprechaun,
I can wish on either of two new moons,
Billboards are graven with mystic runes,
Shirts hung to dry are ragtag gypsies,
Mud puddles loom like Mississipsies,
And billiard balls resemble plums,
And street lamps are chrysanthemums.
If my vision were twenty-twenty,
I should miss miracles a-plenty.

YOU CAN BE A REPUBLICAN,
I'M A GEROCRAT

Oh, "rorty" was a mid-Victorian word
Which meant "fine, splendid, jolly,"
And often to me it has reoccurred
In moments melancholy.
For instance, children, I think it rorty
To be with people over forty.

I can't say which, come eventide,
More tedious I find;
Competing with the juvenile stride,
Or meeting the juvenile mind.
So I think it rorty, yes, and nifty,
To be with people over fifty.

The pidgin talk the youthful use
Bypasses conversation.
I can't believe the code they choose
Is a means of communication.
Oh to be with people over sixty
Despite their tendency to prolixty!

The hours a working parent keeps
Mean less than Latin to them,
Wherefore they disappear in jeeps
Till three and four A.M.

Oh, to be with people you pour a cup for
Instead of people you have a wait up for!

I've tried to read young mumbling lips
Till I've developed a slant-eye,
And my hearing fails at the constant wails
Of, If I can't, why can't I?
Oh, to be beside a septuagenarian,
Silent upon a peak in Darien!

They don't know Hagen from Bobby Jones,
They never heard Al Smith,
Even Red Grange is beyond their range,
And Dempsey is a myth.
Oh golly, to gabble upon the shoulder
Of someone my own age, or even older!

I'm tired of defining hadn't oughts
To opposition mulish,
The thoughts of youth are long long thoughts,
And Jingo! Aren't they foolish!
All which is why, in case you've wondered
I'd like a companion aged one hunderd.

CROSSING THE BORDER

Senescence begins
And middle age ends
The day your descendants
Outnumber your friends.

CROSS WITH
THE DOCTOR?

OR, LET'S PROVOKE A FEW
ROUND HIPPOCRATIC OATHS

WHAT THE WELL-READ
PATIENT IS TALKING ABOUT
OR, LOOK MA, WHAT I GOT!

The more I leaf through the dictionary in my physician's
    waiting room the more my ego grows;
I feel rather like the man who was delighted to find that
    all his life he had been speaking prose,
Because I discover that my modest minor ailments,
Why, when expressed in scientific terminology, they are
    major physical derailments.
What I thought were merely little old mumps and measles
    turn out to have been parotitis and rubella,
And chicken pox, that's for the birds, have I told you
    about my impressive varicella?
I apologize for my past solecisms, which were heinous,
Never again shall I mention flat feet or bunions when
    referring to the hallux valgus on my pes planus.
It projects me into a state of hypnosis
To reflect that a watched pot never boils, it furunculosis.
Once my internal rumblings at parties caused me to wish
    I could shrink to nothing, or at least to a pigmy,
But now I proudly inquire, Can everybody hear my
    borborygmi?
My one ambition is to become as rich as Croesus.
So that instead of this bourgeois backache I can afford
    some spondylolisthesis,

Although then I suppose I would look back on my im-
    pecunious days with acute nostalgia
Because my headaches would also have progressed from
    rags to riches, or from Horatio Alger to cephalalgia.
I have certainly increased my learning by more than a
    smidgin,
Now I know that that specifically projecting Hollywood
    starlet is not a squab, she's a steatopigeon.
Indeed, I know so much that it would be truly tragic were
    I to be afflicted with aphasia,
And if you can't swallow that statement it is my diagnosis
    that you are suffering from achalasia.

COUSIN EUPHEMIA
KNOWS BEST
OR, PHYSICIAN, HEAL SOMEBODY ELSE

Some people don't want to be doctors because they think
    doctors have to work too hard to make a living,
And get called away from their bed at night and from
    their dinner on Christmas and Thanksgiving.
These considerations do not influence me a particle;
I do not want to be a doctor simply because somewhere in
    the family of every patient is a female who has read
    an article.
You remove a youngster's tonsils and the result is a
    triumph of medical and surgical science,
He stops coughing and sniffling and gains eleven pounds
    and gets elected captain of the Junior Giants,
But his great-aunt spreads the word that you are a quack,
Because she read an article in the paper last Sunday
    where some Rumanian savant stated that tonsillec-
    tomy is a thing of the past and the Balkan hospitals
    are bulging with people standing in line to have
    their tonsils put back.
You suggest calamine lotion for the baby's prickly heat,
And you are at once relegated to the back seat,
Because its grandmother's cousin has seen an article in the
    "Household Hints" department of *Winning Par-
    cheesi* that says the only remedy for prickly heat is
    homogenized streptomycin,

And somebody's sister-in-law has seen an article where
   the pathologist of *Better Houses and Trailers* says
   calamine lotion is out, a conscientious medicine man
   wouldn't apply calamine lotion to an itching bison.
I once read an unwritten article by a doctor saying there
   is only one cure for a patient's female relative who
   has read an article:
A hatpin in the left ventricle of the hearticle.

MS FOUND IN A QUAGMIRE

Up, up, lad, time's a-wastin', press the ignition.
If relief is not forthcoming, consult your physician.
Winnow your symptoms, but never discard the chaff,
And consult your physician, your physician deserves a
    laugh.
Explain that when you swallow so much as a coddled egg
    it sticks like a fishbone
Somewhere behind your wishbone;
Inquire why your eyes of a sudden refuse to be focused,
And what is the sound in your ears like a courting locust.
Your physician's a man of talents;
Ask him whatever became of your sense of balance.
Don't be irked by his suavity;
Tell how you walk with your legs braced wide lest you
    trip over gravity;
Tell him, too, that your gaze is fixed on your shoes as you
    walk, and better to tell him why:
That a too long upward glance would send you headlong
    into the sky.
Tell him straight that on such and such a day
They took the difference between down and up away.
Give him your problem to solve,
Ask him what to hold onto when under your feet you can
    feel the earth revolve;
Every molehill a mountain, every wormhole a crater,

And every step like the step at the top of the escalator,
And don't forget
To reveal your discovery that hair can sweat.
Go ahead, tell him;
Release the cat from the bag, let the doctor bell him.
Give the doctor the chart, show him the map and the
     graph;
If relief is not forthcoming, it says right here on the label,
     consult your physician, your physician deserves a
     laugh.

I YIELD TO MY LEARNED
BROTHER
OR, IS THERE A CANDLESTICK MAKER
IN THE HOUSE?

The doctor gets you when you're born,
The preacher, when you marry,
And the lawyer lurks with costly clerks
If too much on you carry.
Professional men, they have no cares;
Whatever happens, they get theirs.

You can't say When
To professional men,
For it's always When to they;
They go out and golf
With the big bad wolf
In the most familiar way.
Hard times for them contain no terrors;
Their income springs from human errors.

The noblest lord is ushered in
By a practicing physician,
And the humblest lout is ushered out
By a certified mortician.
And in between, they find their foyers
Alive with summonses from lawyers.

[113]

Oh, would my parents long ago
Had memorized this motto!
For then might I, their offspring, buy
A Rolls or an Isotto.
But now I fear I never can,
For I am no professional man.

You can't say When
To professional men,
For it's always When to they;
They were doing fine
In '29,
And they're doing fine today.
One beacon doth their paths illumine,
To wit: To err is always humine.

ARTHUR

There was an old man of Calcutta,
Who coated his tonsils with butta,
Thus converting his snore
From a thunderous roar
To a soft, oleaginous mutta.

THE STRANGE CASE OF THE
LUCRATIVE COMPROMISE

Some people are in favor of compromising, while other
    people to compromise are loath.
I cannot plump for either side, I think there is something
    to be said for both.
But enough of discussion, let us proceed to example,
Of which the experience of Porteous Burnham should be
    ample.
The infant Burnham was a prodigious phenomenon, a
    phenomenon truly prodigious,
His parents and teachers regarded him with awe verging
    on the religious.
His genius was twofold, it appeared to have no ceiling,
And it was directed toward the science of lexicography
    and the science of healing.
Anatomy and etymology were Pablum to the infant Burn-
    ham;
At the age of five he knew that people don't sit down on
    their sternum,
Although he would occasionally say so in jest,
Later explaining that the word derived from the Greek
    sternon, meaning chest.
At the age of twenty-one he was an M.D. and a D.Litt.,
    but his career hung in the balance,
Because he couldn't choose between his talents,

Until one day he was approached by an advertising agency that had heard of his dual gift,

And to work out a compromise they made shift,

And now he is the one who thinks up those frightening pseudo-scientific names for all the strange new ailments the consumer gets —

That is, if he uses some other sponsor's toothpaste or cigarettes;

And he makes a hundred thousand dollars a year, U.S. not Mexican,

Because the compromise landed him in a luxurious penthouse on Park Avenue, which is midway between Medicine and Lexicon.

MUCH BETTER,
THANK YOU

WHEN THE DEVIL WAS SICK
COULD HE PROVE IT?

Few things are duller
Than feeling unspecifically off-color,
Yes, you feel like the fulfillment of a dismal phophecy,
And you don't feel either exercisey or officey,
But still you can't produce a red throat or a white tongue
    or uneasy respiration or any kind of a symptom,
And it is very embarrassing that whoever was supposed
    to be passing out the symptoms skymptom,
Because whatever is the matter with you, you can't spot
    it
But whatever it is, you've got it,
But the question is how to prove it,
And you suck for hours on the thermometer you finally
    sent out for and you can't move it,
And your entire system may be pneumococci'd or strep-
    tococci'd,
But the looks you get from your loved ones are simply
    skeptococci'd,
So you unfinger your pulse before Conscience can jeer at
    you for a compulsive fingerer,
And you begin to believe that perhaps your loved ones
    are right, perhaps you are nothing but a hypochon-
    driacal old malingerer,
And you take a farewell look at the thermometer, and it's
    as good as a tonic,

[120]

Because you've got as pretty a ninety-nine point one as
    you'd wish to see in a month of bubonic.
Some people hold out for a hundred or more before they
    collapse
But that leaves too many gaps;
As for me,
I can get a very smug Monday, Tuesday, Wednesday,
    Thursday, or Friday in bed out of a tenth of a
    degree.
It is to this trait that I am debtor
For the happy fact that on weekends I generally feel
    better.

NO DOCTORS TODAY,
THANK YOU

They tell me that euphoria is the feeling of feeling won-
    derful, well, today I feel euphorian,
Today I have the agility of a Greek god and the appetite
    of a Victorian.
Yes, today I may even go forth without my galoshes,
Today I am a swashbuckler, would anybody like me to
    buckle any swashes?
This is my euphorian day,
I will ring welkins and before anybody answers I will
    run away.
I will tame me a caribou
And bedeck it with marabou.
I will pen me my memoirs.
Ah youth, youth! What euphorian days them was!
I wasn't much of a hand for the boudoirs,
I was generally to be found where the food was.
Does anybody want any flotsam?
I've gotsam.
Does anybody want any jetsam?
I can getsam.
I can play chopsticks on the Wurlitzer,
I can speak Portuguese like a Berlitzer.
I can don or doff my shoes without tying or untying the
    laces because I am wearing moccasins,

And I practically know the difference between serums
    and antitoccasins.
Kind people, don't think me purse-proud, don't set me
    down as vainglorious,
I'm just a little euphorious.

WHAT TO DO UNTIL
THE DOCTOR GOES
OR, IT'S TOMORROW THAN YOU THINK

Oh hand me down my old cigar with its Havana wrap-
per and its filling of cubeb,
Fill the little brown jug with bismuth and paregoric, and
the pottle and cannikin with soda and rhubeb,
Lend me a ninety-nine piece orchestra tutored by Kousse-
vitsky,
I don't want the ownership of it, I just want the use-
vitsky,
Bring me a firkin of Arkansas orators to sing me ora-
torios,
Remove these calf-clad Spenglers and Prousts and re-
place them with paper-covered Wodehouses and
Gaboriaus,
Wrap up and return these secretarial prunes and prisms,
Let me have about me bosoms without isms.
Life and I are not convivial,
Life is real, life is earnest, while I only think I am real,
and know I am trivial.
In this imponderable world I lose no opportunity
To ponder on picayunity.
I would spend either a round amount or a flat amount
To know whether a puma is only tantamount to a cata-
mount or paramount to a catamount,

It is honey in my cup,
When I read of a sprinter sprinting the hundred in ten
    seconds flat, to think: Golly, suppose he stood up!
No, I am not delirious, just aglow with incandescence;
This must be convalescence.

I WILL ARISE AND GO NOW

In far Tibet
There live a lama,
He got no poppa,
Got no momma,

He got no wife,
He got no chillun,
Got no use
For penicillun,

He got no soap,
He got no opera,
He don't know Geritol
From copra,

Got no opinions
Controversial,
He never hear
TV commercial,

He got no teeth,
He got no gums,
Don't eat no Spam,
Don't need no Tums.

He love to nick him
When he shave;

He also got
No hair to save.

Got no distinction,
No clear head,
Don't call for Calvert;
Drink milk instead.

He use no lotions
For allurance,
He got no car
And no insurance,

No Alsop warnings,
No Reston rumor
For this self-centered
Nonconsumer.

Indeed, the
Ignorant Have-Not
Don't even know
What he don't got.

If you will mind
The box-tops, comma,
I think I'll go
And join that lama.